To Marguerite,
our "open En[d]
with pleasure.
Love Olivia

JOYCE — A CLEW

Published by Bluett and Company Limited 1981

ISBN 0 907899 00 5

Designed by Bluett and Company Limited.
Set in Palatino type
and printed at The Northern Press, Dublin.

JOYCE
-A CLEW

BLUETT AND COMPANY LIMITED
DUBLIN

WHEN WE DEAD AWAKEN

TOWARDS the close of the last century, the shadow of Parnell cast gloom over Ireland. Patriots wore ivy perfectly black. The last chair had been pushed back in Committee Room Fifteen. The laments of the outcasts echoed through the long corridors of a Parliament abandoned forever. The Chief was dead. The mournful face of the martyred leader stared accusation from the walls of bourgeois drawing-rooms. The Uncrowned King of Ireland held sway over ghosts and myth once displaced history to forge a new reality.

Charles Stewart Parnell was an over-reacher. Arrogant and contemptuous, he jousted with fate and dared his people to betray him. Idolised by the peasantry, he remained aloof. Tolerated by the Church, he forced his hand. A danger to England, he stood alone and lost the game. The party which he schooled too well chose Home Rule before dictatorship. The Tin God tumbled. Quicklime flew in Castlecomer. Cassocked eunuchs brayed denouncements from the pulpit. The deer was brought to bay and sacrificed upon the altar of morality. The parasites moved on.

In February 1882, a child was born to Charles Parnell and Katharine, wife of Captain William Henry O'Shea. The child did not survive. But in the same month, another attempted entry and succeeded. For him, Ireland's damp and misty climate of grandiose romanticism was ideal. He did not know the name of hesitency. He could defend the heel of any hero. James Augusta Joyce would flourish.

THE BALLAD OF JOKING JESUS

WHILE the Cardinals played Borgia and Lucrezia unloosed once more her jaded finery, Old Father Church pursued the latest son of Eireann. Senile, hung with purple velvet and weighted by the chain of His High Office, he arrived early at the christening to grant the child the legacy of an ancient reign of terror. The Holy Roman Catholic and Apostolic Church does not tantalise with promises. Unlike the sons of Zion, the servants of Babylon can lay no claim to household godship. Rome barters for the soul. Her blessings are a threat. The price of sin is Hell Fire. The heretic burns for all eternity while life can be whispered into dust within the dark confessional. This then was James' joyless inheritance.

But Palestrina sounds a more seductive note. Behind the Pillars of the Church, the steward of the Lord gains eminence. Virgin, bathed in sweet stained glass light and clad in sacred vestments, the priest conducts his sacred ceremony. By twilight, the Reverend Stephen Dedalus S.J. could verse himself in subtle wisdom. At night, he could walk coldly through the catacombs of Vatican intrigue. In sleep, he could lay down his untouched head upon a bed of thorns and dream of earthly paradise. But this Stephen preferred the martyrdom of Art. He would uncover his own universe of profane mystery. He could not serve another's God.

Like Lucifer, James Joyce demanded choice. If the price of freedom was banishment, so be it. He must be Lord and Master of his soul. In solitary splendour, his promethean paean would resound. Poor Old Nick was closer the the angels than appears.

THE PRODIGAL SON

JOHN Joyce, ebullient and extravagant, resolved his eldest son should have the best education that Ireland could offer. So James was sent down along the River Liffey to be apprenticed to the Jesuits at Clongowes Wood.

Within three years, he was recalled. The days of Christmas partying and gentleman's agreements were almost over for the Joyce ménage. While Mother groaned and Father wept, bad debt accumulated.

The business life of Joyce Pater made good fiction but little else. He had raised his glass too often in toast to a dead king and ten children overstrained his slender budget.

Thus commenced a Dublin Odyssey. Mortgage followed mortgage and the urban map was studded with Joyce Halls of Residence. While John bloomed full in chaos, wife May prayed for rest.

From school to school and street to street, Sunny Jim retained his place beside the hearth of home. Apostate or no, the wayward son was not denied his freedom. The constancy of mother love was swayed alone by death, a first and last abandonment.

The lessons learnt at mother's knee were honoured but scarce developed. Dreamy Jimmy elaborated only on direct experience. Maternity defies a man. And woman is synonym of treason.

Hamlet Joyce courted his father's spirit through the maze of many cities. John's endless tales and sentimental songs were rationed out among one hundred characters. His son reserved the demons for himself.

Hopping and trotting about Europe, Joyce nimbly skipped Bohemia, approaching burgherhood in his fondness of family. For him the gathering of clans was of supreme importance and portraits of Joyce generations fortified his walls.

His life achieved its zenith with paternity. He baffled his two children with strange maternal love. A rebel son of Church and State, Joyce reserved the human right to sing a father's lullaby.

ELEGANT AND ANTIQUE PHRASE

AMDG

LONG long ago, on the banks of fair flowing Boyne, a boy tended a fish for his master. All his days the old man had sought after the Salmon of Knowledge and now it turned before him on the spit, sizzling with the promise of omniscience. He smiled as he awaited the taste of triumph. But he was presumptuous. Fate granted the prize to the servant. The child reached out to claim his destiny and Finn MacCumhal ruled over all wise men.

Great deeds of glory followed and the fame of Finn was fabled through the world. Time passed and like every mortal man the mighty hero too grew old. His strength ebbed and as he came to broken age his kingdom fell to ruins. He saw his laughing wife and most beloved son betray him but he could act no more. Saxon invaders ruled the land and cast him into shame. In vain he mumbled at the Bench of Justice in language sad and ancient.

At last the few remaining warriors of Fál heard music in his words. They swore to avenge the weeping leader with the thunder of their guns. But Finn's honour was past saving and the men of Ireland perished in attempt. All hope of conquest crumbled and the myth of Finn lived only in the mad meanderings of night-time storytellers.

Until one day in a soft morning city at the ford of the two hurdles another boy pricked up his ears. He heard the voice of Finn whispering in the waters of a greater river. He listened close to clod and pebble and built up a new armoury of words. And when he had rephrased the son of Finn he sang it to all tyrants. He harmonized with neither Boyne nor Avon. Intelligible to all and none he lauded Joy and Genesis.

LDS

IN DUBLIN'S FAIR CITY

THE capital of Ireland spread itself at Joyce's feet. He wandered without rest between and far beyond the two canals of Dublin. Every lane's end, every shop, church, session, hanging, every vice and every virtue yielded its lush crop to his hot brain. Coveting his neighbour's word and keeping tally on his fingers, he learned the town by heart. He would gather, order and present complete the city of his birth to Europe.

Once seen, the picture held. When Joyce retired to memory, he did not lose his way. He made a labyrinth of Dublin and signposted each part. Flesh and blood were shifted wholesale into print. He stalked the Minotaur of Time through the dead-ends of paralysis. Joyce stopped the clock.

When the city spawned an alter ego, conflict was inevitable. While Joyce produced his portraits, his models drank in pubs. And talked. Many held it was not honesty to be thus transubstantiated. Great rivalry developed between fact and fiction.

But the citizens of Dublin solved the Joyce dilemma. They died, discarding all originals. Destruction pushes onward. Still the ghostly masterbuilder, being blind, picks his path among the debris and raises up a fallen city. The shade of Stephen forever goes the rounds of Vico Road, calmly intoning the book of himself. Having brought forth a world in his own image, Herr Satan becomes God.

So one Dublin disappears into a book. The door of Seven Eccles Street leads only to the Blooms. James Joyce alone can own the keys to this vanished city although guidebooks now are peddled in the bursar's rooms of yet another town. Properly deloused by time, Joyce could perhaps be pitied and forgiven.

But he dares still further. Present continuous does not satisfy. He juggles with the future. Clairvoyant, circular, creative, the serpent bites hard on his own tail.

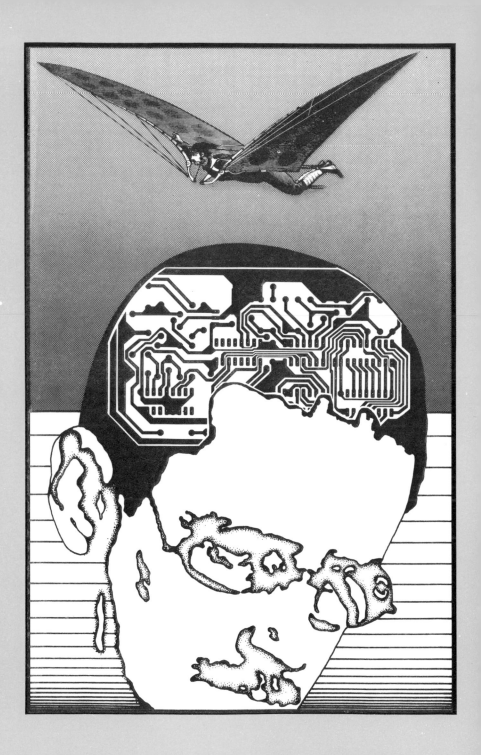

TO ROVE AND RUMMAGE

JAMES Joyce soon grew too large for Dublin. He longed to roam abroad to test his soul and city against a grander backdrop. Buffeted by many winds, he hungered for release. He heard the voice of prophets call him to his Father's Business. His throat ached to invoke Dedalus, to declare himself a Chosen One, to send up a cry of exultation, to fly into the sun.

Old Dedalus, the patron saint of craftsmen, laid aside his instruments to study this new acolyte who struggled with such fervour to achieve the High Priesthood of Art. The Fabulous Artificer, Inventor of Puzzles, Self-Made Exile and Cuckolder of Kings smiled and wondered which of his two sons the Young Pretender would usurp. How the little fellow flashed his antlers! Yet his courage deserved praise.

Ulysses of the Nimble-Wits paused also to observe. He too had once left land and duty to adventure through the world to sound all worth and wickedness. He recognised the errant Dubliner and approved his explorations.

Joyce did not linger long on these Parnassian slopes. Brilliance flaunted, he flung himself headlong into the temporal. To fill his lungs, to plunge in sin, to fail and triumph, to create life from life. Like Homer, all his gods grow human.

Perched high upon the utmost peak of Mont Olympus, where he had no right to be, the Prince of Darkness surveyed his now lost protégé. Another flash in the pan of doubt. The Spearshaker was once quite promising but ended up the right hand man of God. His Intensity would mellow too. He shook his head morosely and turned to gaze on the more solid satisfactions of policeman and itinerant outside the ProCathedral.

THE MUMMERS

AS Joyce prepared his coming forth by day, others were returning into mist. Higher and holier enlightenment lay onwards yet his countrymen regressed.

The broken lights of myth were flickering and Yeats reopened an old path through bog and treachery.

When Joyce knocked at the door, the Irish Literary Movement did not recognise its star performer.

Yeats was preoccupied with Irish Stew and James soon lost his appetite. He bowed to his host's imagination but refused to share his table.

Walking as he did through the light of his vocation, Joyce had scant interest in a Celtic pot of broth. Besides, he would bask in no man's reflected glory.

It was the hard cold light of Europe that drew him on. Not the squint in Irish eyes. Nor twalette that was neither night nor day.

Ibsen's messenger announced his presence. Yeats was polite but unabashed. Himself engaged in a great journey, the poet could offer help but little sympathy.

Joyce despised the Yeats scenario. He would find no converts here. Abbey Street led straight to Lobsterland.

He had enough of Ireland before Ireland had enough of him. He was not martyred although he needed martyrdom. He called for marching orders.

Yet he was no Croppy Boy. His words would send no young men to their deaths. For him desire was all.

Half-man, half-god, he freed himself of fetters. The denizens of demi-art could never catch this hero.

The seeker after truth can call no man his fellow. The rabblement cannot provide him company. Nor can it thwart him.

Joyce filched material from every quarrel and styled himself a pair of wings. Taking what he needed, he left the dross behind.

He made and remade reasons for departure. Before sunrise on the Continent, Ireland turned her back. His cue was apathy.

At war with both censor and censored, he issued ultimata. The artist preaches for himself alone. He must choose isolation.

This then was Joycean exile.

ON LOOKING FOR THE LOAN OF A TANNER

Alas, life did not treat our hero kindly when he first began to sojourn on the Continent. Full many times the faithful husband and proud father was forced by circumstance to pawn all his trumpery to keep his brood from starving. Who can blame him if he oft became dejected and resorted to the consolation of the wine-shop? Among the strolling players and rogues of low degree, he could strengthen his high purpose.

Exhausted by the mighty struggle, at last he called for help. His younger brother, one Stanislaus, received the word. He did not tarry but abandoning all thought of self he sped through many countries to share his bread and cheese. And yet Dame Fortune led the household on a merry dance.

In misery, the poet auctioned off his talents in the schools and offices of Europe. He slid up balustrades to amuse young ladies and down again to patch his borrowed britches. From town to town he hawked his ballads, magic-lantern shows and finery but all to no avail. And when by candlelight he sat down to puzzle-contests, he lamented the lost days of youth when he brought his father sailing on the Irish Sea with money earned from scholarship.

Over the slow years, his fame began to grow. Through all his trials, the savant wrote and wrote till news of his sad plight reached to the shores of Albion. There damsels Pound and Yeats petitioned to the King and Shem was summoned to account. He dazzled all with calculations and touched the hardest heart. The rich ladies and new freewomen of the court were charmed and showered gold upon him. Penmen everywhere donated pence and sent their cast-off clothing.

Until the evening of his days, the bold bard fought with finance. Few paid him for his poems and many pirated his work. Each volume that he wrote cost far more to produce than he ever gained from it. Extravagance and penury vied continually for favour — for if the truth be known he was a wily spendthrift. And when now, in the comfort of the night, the Man from Monte Carlo rose up to sing his anthem still was much more spirited than most.

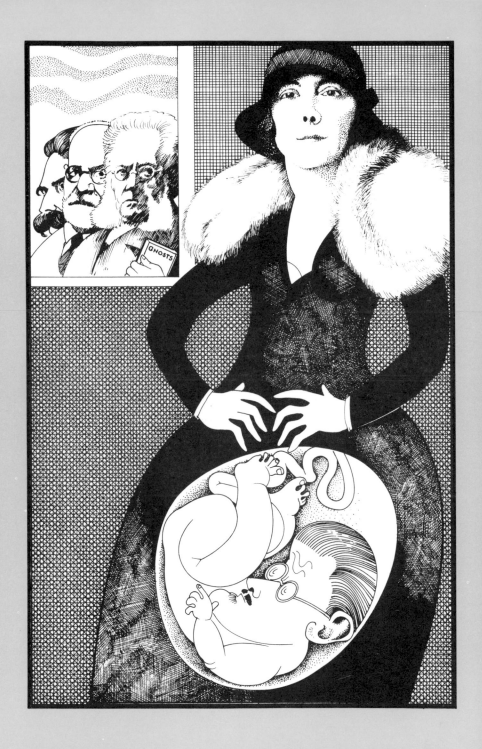

GHOSTS

DARK ROSALEEN

THE Joyce who spent his youth hailholyqueening about town between benediction and the brothel could not forgo fulfilment. The atmosphere of mountain peaks was too rarefied for life. Man must, to gain wholeness, pursue the dark and shameful shade of womanhood. Jesus forfeits his humanity when he ignores the female. His lady madonnas warp and weary passion and courtly love grows sterile. By turning his face towards fresh air, Joyce intended to embrace the Sin of Man more than symbolically. The carnal mysteries became his new Magnificat. Alluring, fertile, amoral, woman draws the artist into creativity. Sex is the human sacrament. In that moment of transfiguration, the boy becomes a man.

Nora Barnacle calmly challenged church, standards and society when she chose to associate herself with Joyce. A casual encounter in Nassau Street led to years of rootless wandering. Her heart rose to meet adventure. The life-long loyalty which she maintained to partnership makes mad music of Joycean hyperbole. The boy-man did not set out for exile quite unfellowed, friendless and alone. It was an embassy of two.

Joyce weaves a subtle tapestry of man's interrelationship with man. He unveils a panorama of male consciousness. His woman is a simpler creature. She can be presented generically. As wife and tender consort, she assuages loneliness. Profound in her indifference, she can subdue, sustain, produce, betray according to temptation. As great sweet mother, matron evercomforting and forgiving, she lies at the very base of nature. Primeval, she supports all the schemings of mankind. Less obvious, as intellectual, she is an awkward hybrid. She can recognise the talents of her brother and nurture him as son. The net of patriarchy defied Joyce to pass in flight. He tangled in its coils. Ecce Homo. Mona Lisa smiles.

WHO GOES WITH FERGUS

ART is morality. The insubordination of James Joyce implies no lapse. The artist must assume responsibility for his life and work. It is inevitable that Joyce replaces vows of obedience with supreme and personal faith. Extrication is a prerequisite of examination. He approaches the world with curiosity and expresses without compromise all that he uncovers. His art is affirmation and he elevates his own position only because of this absolute commitment to a truth. Artistic honesty entails both fearless proclamation of one's view and relentless pursuit of perfection in a craft. Technique no less than ideals determines morality in art. The stringent application of such principles is more ethical than arrogant.

The self-imposed isolation of Joyce was both inspired and tempered by his close identification with Henrik Ibsen. The Doktor's integrity and aloof authority provided him with a model. The wilful selfishness of both shielded the monumental moral courage which they also shared. Joyce did not mark the trolls' response to his indictments. His cries of joy were uttered into immense incertitude. He would not curtail his freedom to pander or explain.

By asserting individuality, Joyce aims at universals. His stigmata of opposed contraries yield coincidence not conflict. The rebel who disdains to serve becomes his own taskmaster. Heresiarchs defy theology to create another conscience. A language which is alien can be renewed uniquely. The exile who takes his city into exile with him echoes the logic of a homeland where absence is generally the highest form of presence. Every anarchist makes whole a disunited kingdom. Truth is disclosed in paradox.

DIVINE COMEDIAN

IN the beginning there was Chaos and Chaos begat Tumult and Tumult begat Terror and Terror begat God and God begat Order and Order begat Restraint and Restraint begat Joyce and Joyce begat Chaos.

It so happened that this James, surnamed Joyce, having murdered all the makers of old saws and fled from the Land of Youth to the Mount of Godlessness, began to weary of his lonesome state and pine for further challenge.

It came to pass that he chanced to glance down from the heights to see the Earth beneath. The wealth of Human Life astounded him and, as in a dream, it was revealed to him that Absolutes were Obsolete — the Banal becomes Portentous.

With haste he descended to the Valley, a Golden Calf no more but Everyman. He chose a wife and sired children and vowed to crisscross all experience from Bell and Book to Candle.

Heathen, Turk and Jew became One to him. He allowed all to share a Common Nature although he did not scruple to deck each out in Local Name and Habitation. For to love at all a man must love himself.

But this Arnolfini suffered from a Fatal Flaw. The Son of Doubt can never know the names of Time and Space and Resolution. All that he gazed upon became divided and system yielded to Confusion and Schism rent his reason.

Thus he grew a very Janus and with monstrous double-vision refracted images of self into eternity. All Joyce became the Universe and the Universe became all Joyce.

Then he withdrew once more from Man to plunder past and present. He heaped up detail on the crack most cunningly to hide it. He saw the blackbird thirteen ways and gave a voice to each. With Shapes and Signs and Superstitions, he etched out his Holy Books. By virtue of Absurdity, he outcreated God,

And when he saw his work complete, the Earth resounded to the Thunder of his Laugh. Know ye that this be Truth and that this Laughter rings the world without end forever and ever Amen.

A ROW AND A RUCTION

CHARGES against a Dublin man, who stood accused of threatening public morality and libelling his fellow citizens, were adjourned yesterday pending further investigation.

The man, James Augustine Joyce B.A., of no fixed abode, at first refused to plead but then denied before the High Court that his books were in any way obscene. He claimed to be a "serious artist" and said that he wrote down "only what he saw".

Common Sewer

Judge H.C. Rumbold questioned the accuracy of Mr. Joyce's eyesight and expressed surprise that a man educated by the Jesuits could not direct his attention beyond the common sewer.

Mr. Joyce, who conducted his own defence, disrupted court proceedings by presenting his case in a language later identified as Dano-Norwegian. Judge Rumbold cautioned the defendant for his "smartness" and said that he would be found in contempt if he did not tender due respect to the Queen's English.

Public Enemy

Mr. Joyce then stated that he would not be bullied and said that he resented being hounded as a public enemy when in fact he was the only honest man then present in the courtroom.

"I am only a simple middle-class man", he said, and added that his attempt to "purge the conscience of his race" was made in all good faith. He suggested that the intelligence of the general reader was in many ways deficient.

Bonfires

Opening the case for the prosecution, Mr. T. M. Healy submitted that the defendant's heresy was well-known. He could find neither publisher nor printer for his slander. His books were banned in Britain and America and had twice made up a pretty bonfire.

The defendant protested at this juncture and alleged that he approached his art in a spirit of "great reverence". He said his heart was broken with continual litigation and he wanted only "to live in peace"

Questionable Elements

Witnesses for the defence testified that Mr. Joyce was "a pillar of the community" and "a harmless poor eejit". Questionable elements in his work must be understood in context. There were shouts of "Filth" and "Turncoat" from the Public Gallery.

Judge Rumbold said the case disturbed him more than any he had heard in many a day. He said that any slur on the honour of the Irish people would meet with the full rigours of the law.

The trial continues today.

? ¿ DADA ?

DADA

children may just as well play as not.

the ogre will come in any case.

dada h !

SHILLELAGH LAW

WRATH roars across the dome of earth pushing sulphur clouds of massy black apart against the tumult of infernal night to bare the fury of red raging hellfire spewing fast with hate to rape the heavens and sweep in lethal onslaught to savage the horizon. Luna is hurled molten from her place before the thunder's rage and ghastly Zeus sent spinning wildly groans and bleeds into one million vicious arrows to scourge the flesh of humankind. Flayed by relentless rain, maddened and caught helpless in a howling mortal folly, the ranked formations of demented man split in terror — scatter — swarm — shriek a tortured swansong of despair into angry space. The Tree of Life is rent in twain. The Raven shoots into oblivion. Darkness swallows all.

Beneath the white and cobalt skies of neutral Zürich, each man cultivates his garden. The lake shimmers in the sun, snaking forth among the waters of slow Limmat to touch the peaceful town. Carrying the tang of pinewood from the hills, the Föhn freshens citizens. Burghers go about good business and guildsmen hone and polish age-old crafts. The marketplace is thriving although supplies are short.

In cafe and restaurant at evening the spies of Europe congregate. The conspirators take a separate stand but shout loud to their neighbours. They talk of battles fought and won behind the forehead, bitter conflict with contempt and daily bouts with falsehood. They hold contests of old wounds. One chased a nimble Greek through twenty thousand hours before he captured him. Another spent a night of sixteen years in Lethe and forfeited his sight. A third, tied to a mast, had his back bent double to recreate the music of the spheres. O take the laurel crown.

A thin man in dark glasses sits in a corner and strokes a calm tiger. He hears a vendor crying news of Guernica and turning to a Russian émigré he breaks a lifelong silence.

"Who won this war", he says.

the Duc de Joyeux dances

THE MINSTREL BOY

he was whirling dervish at the dancing right enough you'd
wonder what fuel he had in him at all there he'd be all day long
writing out his stuff in letters big enough to see a mile away his
life was no bed of roses really but once the night would start he'd
be off gallivanting round the town there was no stopping him

he'd sit in bistros drinking sparkling wine and talk his head off
to anyone that had the time to listen and there were plenty of
those too god knows how they stuck it there he'd be mouthing all
the words he liked and didn't like in forty languages and getting
everyone to say what a lovely sound they had as if they cared
regaling them with stories and singing songs till all hours
ireland's answer to caruso he was meant to be

he wasn't strong either come to think of it though you'd never
guess it by the antics out of him when you'd see him coming
with his glittering eyes you'd need to sidestep pretty quick
before he buttonholed you and want to do you favours or want
you to do him favours you'd never know which with the
cuteness out of him

then he'd drag you off to meet the wife and children and he'd be
cutting capers on the street when you'd be putting matchsticks in
your eyes you were that deadbeat but you'd have to play along
for fear he'd put you in the book and ruin you completely his
mountain flower he called her though that was nice

and once he'd have you home he'd be forcing drink on you and
getting you to tell him your opinions till he'd get his second
wind and start prancing round the room like some grasshoper
gone crazy whirling round his arms and making funny faces until
you'd be afraid he'd fall what with all the furniture and his
eyesight being so bad and next thing you'd know the cut glass
would be shining in a heap of diamonds on the floor and him
among them laughing

still he had his good points i suppose

THE BOOK OF INNOVATIONS

TO see the mad monk work upon his midnight magic book was marvel beyond durance. With seven tongues in seven cheeks, he synchronised a world. There, beside the green-barked yew, he bound his sheets of vellum. His questioning was never quelled till quill and ink had freed him. Philosophy was not his sport, though paradox much pleased him. Sensation was this seer's love, as in the time of sages. He crushed his colours out of earth and conjured countless wonders. Gold-vermillion bloomed his text with letters of wine-red. Crimson plucked from wayside blossom stained the rubric of this verse. Carnelian and golden-rod glowed eerie from those pages. How emerald and glauconite, embossed the spider-writing. Meticulous, he bent to task, to graft the bones of metrics. With rimes spun round, four-harmonied, he wrestled stubbornly. Till there he bowed down at the altar abstracting arabesques. With bodkins, braces, beetles, bores, chasers, cockscrews, circles, crabs, crayons, crankshafts, chisels, chalk, dibbles, dovetails, dados, donkeys, hacksaws, headers, jigsaws, jointers, Yes, pitchforks, planers, pulpers, pancakes, ratchets, crotchets, gimlets, grindstones, monkeys, shapers, slotters, stag gangs, wimbles, filters, fingers, microns, barrels, quadrants, sextants, transits, prisms, elbows, ellmen, finders, keepers, pseudos, sleepers, snipers, snoopers, sinners more. These are the tools he used to alchemise his verbal atom. Rich was the harvest reaped in his autumnal hide-out. Deep within the cave of memory, these miracles were wrought. He wove a web about his words to yield a gorgeous fabric. Intricate was the path he wound through that enchanted night. Fearless are allmen who follow, to brave his mystery. This zany knew the secret ways of stealth and subterfuge. Playing pattern's paradigm, he puzzled out palimpsests. Blinding is the beauty bared by the scribe of seven scrolls. Silence is the only state can meet that grotesque genius. Stop the breath when you behold the mad monk's machinations.

AT THE MID•HOUR OF NIGHT

FAITH is the first principle. Self-faith freed Joyce of the hopeless burden of denial which fear of death throws up. Death is but a marker of life's profound simplicity. It is as foolish to defend oneself against the end with name-tagged gods as it is to trap worldwonder in a sceptic's net of system. All dogma destroys life. Naked and alone, James Joyce faced the mystery. Having defined his unique function early, his response was celebration.

He held faith with a hidden harmony to affirm all that he saw. He luxuriated in experience. Birth, love and death obsessed him. He recognised a richness there which still evades the servants of convention. Not only did he see, he also sang. His lyricism, his wide-eyed fascinations, his glorying in common nature filled a void of human dignity. Joyce thickened life. This world is ample for the sense and reason of a sane humanity.

Within his mind, he ordered a personal universe, developing the realm of fiction to include previously unmentionable banalities of day-to-day existence. He anticipated death by jumping forward to search out the boundaries of sleep. His language slept, dreamt, roused, danced eternal. It shrugged off description to fling wide the gate of possibility — words seething with tumultuous life, sonorous, bearing no message, becoming that message. The achieve of, the mastery of the thing! His virtuosity terrifies. The pages heave. The last great constant of the human day must evade even the master's pen. Death was the only experience on which he was unable to report. Fore-knowledge must have maddened him. In Zürich, on January 13, 1941, he discharged his final debt.

> *Bedad he revives, see how he rises,*
> *And Finnegan rising from the bed,*
> *Says 'Whirl your liquor round like blazes,*
> *Thunam o'n dhoul, do ye think I'm dead?'*

Drumcondra — Mullingar 1982